INFLUENCE
it's *More* than a Position

WANDA J. MONTGOMERY

Copyright © 2020 Wanda Montgomery

Scriptures marked KJV are taken from the KING JAMES VERSION (KJV): KING JAMES VERSION, public domain.

All rights reserved. No part of this book may be reproduced or transmitted in any form or by any means without written permission from the author.

T.A.L.K. Publishing
5215 North Ironwood Road, Suite 200
Glendale, WI 53217
talkconsulting.net

Influence, It's More Than a Position. -- 1st ed.
ISBN 978-1-952327-09-4
Library of Congress Control Number: 2020910653

Dedication

To the foundation from which I grew; the Cherry, Davis, Gray, and Montgomery families, I thank you.

Because of you - I Am.

I dedicate this book to my children Marcelle and Phillip, Adrian and Chauncey, Candace, our grandchildren, Phillip, Jr., Kamille, and Kye.

I recognize that my life would not be complete without my soul mate, my husband, Floyd. You are the greatest influencer in my life. I love you, eternally...

Contents

Foreword 5
Preface 9
Protect Your Name 13
Be Authentic 29
Invest in Relationships 41
Embrace Opportunities 59
Stay the Course 75
Be Innovative 89
Have Faith 99
References 111
Friends, Family, and Lifetime Relationships 113

Foreword
By Marcelle M. Haddix

The Woman I Call Ma

My Ma and I grew up together. I was born in 1974 in Madison, WI. Story goes that my Ma and Dad met at the University of Wisconsin as college students. My Ma from Milwaukee, Wisconsin; my Dad from Gary, Indiana. As you'll read in the pages that follow, theirs was a short courtship. They met in 1972, dated, got engaged, and then married—all in less than a year. Then, I came along not long after. Newlywed, my Ma, and Dad were young parents. They were getting to know each other, figuring out married life, and becoming parents at the same time. The way I see it, our mother/daughter relationship began at the onset of my Ma becoming a woman.

I recently asked my Ma to share my birth story. I was curious about what she remembered about my birth—what happened, who was there, whether they were good memories or traumatic ones. For a first pregnancy, what she shared seemed uneventful. I was late, so she tried different remedies to speed up the labor. My Dad and my Aunt Felecia were present during my delivery. One thing I learned that surprised me was that my Ma decided to go to the shopping mall in the week after I was born. My grandmother reprimanded her for being out in the streets too soon after giving birth. Coming up, I always understood that a new mother was expected to stay home for at least six weeks after giving birth. So, to learn that my Ma defied this cultural norm and her own mother's warning tickled me. Of course, I had to clarify that she didn't take me, a newborn baby, to the mall—which she didn't. But, I also had to ask her, why did she need to go shopping just days after giving birth? And, how did she even feel energetic and rested enough to go to the mall? This minor detail of my birth story conjured up many thoughts and questions that, for me, resulted in simple answers: my Ma was barely 20 doing what 20-year-olds do; my Ma likes to shop; my Ma will do what she sets her mind to do, and my Ma is human.

Growing up with Ma, I didn't know or understand much about her other than her being my Ma. As a child, my Ma was omnipresent—that is, she was present even when she wasn't there. I heard her voice. Even when she wasn't speaking, her expectations were clear. In our home, my Ma was the nurturer, the rule setter, the caretaker, and the disciplinarian. She cooked our meals, grew food in our backyard garden, sewed our clothes, and decorated and maintained our home. She took us to church—including Sunday school and Bible study. She navigated our education and handled school matters. In our early years as mother and daughter, my Ma was a stay-at-home mom. From her example, I learned a great deal about what it meant for a woman to care for her family and make a house a home.

But, as I was coming of age, my Ma was also evolving as a woman. In some ways, my Ma sacrificed her college education to focus her attention on her new marriage and her young family. However, she never gave up on her dreams or desires for herself. She returned to college when I was in my middle school years. I have fond memories of her studying at night and spending time on the University of Wisconsin Milwaukee campus. She even took a co-curricular course in African dance and would practice her choreography at home. No longer just my Ma, she was a college student—a thinker, a writer, a creator, and a dancer. My Ma did what she set out to do; she earned her college degree. We would celebrate her college and my 8th-grade graduations the same year. My Ma would begin a new professional journey—and I would follow in the path that she set for me.

This book represents yet another example of my Ma doing what she sets out to do—she had the idea to write this book for some time now. As I read through the pages of her life, I was moved with emotion to imagine her as a young Black girl growing up in the housing projects of segregated Milwaukee and coming of age while dealing with challenges that many families face. I learned things about my Ma that helped me to better understand the ins and outs of our own mother/daughter relationship. There were many moments while reading that I thought, I never knew this or I never knew that about my Ma—and what do these new revelations say about me. About us. As she shares her story, I am able to lean into a renewed knowing of my Ma as a human being—with ups and downs, strengths and flaws, sacrifices, and desires. She has experienced hurt, pain, and disappointment. But hers is a story of self-love, motivation, and perseverance. This book affirms her love for me as her first-born daughter and documents many of the lessons I learned while witnessing her journey. And, through each lesson, she offers a framework for women aspiring toward independence, leadership, and success.

Today, when describing my Ma to others, I will often say that she is well known in my hometown of Milwaukee. She is a mover and a shaker. She is a civil servant. She is a leader in our family, in her church, in her profession, and the community. Everybody knows Wanda Montgomery. But, for me, she is the woman I call Ma. We are still growing together. Mother and Daughter. Sisters and Friends...

Preface

I planned to retire in 2020. Before I entered the next season of my life, it was important to me to share my journey of influence and integrity with those destined to be impacted by it.

When I began my writing journey, I hadn't the slightest idea the world would experience the greatest pandemic of my life before the release of my book. Months before my book release, the global pandemic COVID-19 shut the world down. I can tell you for sure that in every principle in this book, and every truth I share, the foundation of my faith has been unwavering even in the midst of unprecedented times. This unexpected global event assured me more than ever that this book was necessary. It doesn't matter what happens around you, if the whole world crumbles – your faith, your character, and your integrity, must be consistent.

Throughout my life, grace has positioned me to stand in places I never dreamed I would be. In some cases, I didn't even deserve or qualify to be there according to societal standards. My life, however, has never been governed by social norms, nor the expectations of others—not even my own. God designed my life, and I've been privileged to walk in surrender to His will.

Through my journey, I've learned:

1. Influence can get you in doors degrees cannot.
2. Relationships are the steps that build a bridge to your future.
3. Everyone matters. The secretary today could be the millionaire influencer tomorrow.
4. Failure may come, but you decide what to do about it.
5. Learning when to transfer your energy is necessary.
6. Life is about making commitments, not contracts.
7. You'll never reap the benefits if you keep quitting.
8. The best lessons are learned through peaks and valleys.
9. When people get in trouble, you don't leave them.
10. Tell the truth, because, at the end of the day, the truth will stand when all else fades.

I want you to be inspired to live life unashamed—one governed by ethics and integrity. The way you live matters. At home, in the community, wherever you are, your life should model integrity. When you live a life governed by integrity, there is no need to worry about your reputation or being ashamed. Integrity is the quality of being honest and having strong moral principles. You can't buy it; it's who you are when no one is watching. Integrity is the DNA of character.

If I'm wrong in how I operate and it comes to my attention, because of integrity, I'm the first to get it straight. I can't afford to let it hinder me.

Have I made mistakes? Absolutely. If I know it, I acknowledge it, and I fix it. When I don't, and I'm made aware of it, I come back and correct it. When people don't want to accept the correction that I'm willing to offer, I release them and move beyond the situation. This includes the emotional attachment and any baggage that goes along with what may have transpired. I understand that it's not something I can control, so I give myself permission to move on.

Our most significant sphere of influence and control is within ourselves, not others. When we master ourselves, it positions us to influence those around us effectively.

Has my life been perfect? Absolutely not. I've been homeless. I've encountered loss, suffered accusations, and various discriminations that challenged the very nature of who I am. I am well acquainted with the struggles of being marginalized as an influential woman of color.

So what do I want you to take away from this book?

I want you to know the power of using all your gifts, not leaving anything on the table. To begin, I want women who, like me, are of a seasoned age to know that you are never too old to do anything your heart desires. I understand there are still gifts in me waiting to be discovered and used. I intend to use each one as I continue learning and growing. Writing this book is one of the gifts I discovered and unwrapped so that my legacy will speak wisdom to those willing to listen.

For younger women in the developmental or transitional stages of life, those parenting small children, or changing careers, I want this book to inspire you to express your God-given inner gifts through a life of integrity and influence.

I've walked in influential circles for decades. Within each circle, my name is synonymous with integrity. It has and always will be. I've committed to myself to never deliberately do anything that will bring shame to my name or that of my legacy. My life speaks for itself and has wonderful things to say. Find yourself in my story. Receive encouragement from my heart.

Wanda

Chapter One

Protect Your Name
Your name is the most valuable thing you'll ever own

"A good name is rather to be chosen than great riches, and loving favour rather than silver and gold." - Proverbs 22:1 (KJV)

When your name comes up in a room, and you're not there, what do people say about you? What do people in your presence think of you? What feelings are associated with your name? What influence does your name carry? Consider this, the first gift received at birth is the breath of life; the second is your name.

Your name matters. Joyce Russell, in her Washington Post article, said, "The greatest connection to a person's identity or their personality is their name, some would say it's the most important word in the world to a person."

If what Joyce Russell states is true, it is necessary to know the meaning of your name. If you can ask the parent who named you where your name came from – ask them. If you can't ask them, do research and find out about your name.

Born to Percy and Bessie Gray, the second of nine children, my parents named me Wanda. My mother loved the name. At the time of my birth, there were many well-known female actresses called Wanda, women who symbolized grace and leadership. The name Wanda was very popular and favored.

Discover the Meaning of Your Name.

It was important to me to know what my name meant so I could live up to it. In doing my research about my name, I learned Wanda has a German origin with various meanings.

One that resonated deeply with me was the "shepherdess." A shepherdess is a female shepherd who keeps sheep together in a flock, protecting and tending to their needs. I can see this characteristic played out in multiple scenarios throughout my life. I've often been the one helping and tending to situations as they arise personally and professionally within my family and my community.

Sheknows.com ascribes the name Wanda to those who desire to work with others, seeing them live in peace and harmony. Typically, excellent in understanding and learning, women bearing the name Wanda are said to be scholars and teachers. When presented with issues, they have an innate ability to see the larger picture. That definition perfectly aligns with many aspects of my own life. My name is Wanda, and I am Wanda.

A good name matters, and the moment you are given the gift of your name, it should be good. It goes without saying; there are scores of people carrying a name given at birth that wasn't good. What someone is called greatly impacts their life and could ultimately negatively shape their future. This should have more parents paying closer attention to the names they place on their child(ren). God changed Abram's name to Abraham and Jacobs's name to Israel. Why? Because the names given at birth did not speak to their God-ordained destinies. God had a plan for both Abram and Jacob, but their names did not express where God wanted to take them or how he planned to use them, so he changed their names.

Growing up, my siblings and I had nicknames. Many of them were assigned by our grandfather, Sylvester Davis, affectionately known as "Peck." I have a sister named after our grandmother, and her nickname was "Grandma." My nickname was "Cookie." As a child, my grandfather would bring an assortment of cookies during his visits. I don't know if it was because I liked cookies more than everyone else, but the name "Cookie" somehow attached to me. Those that knew me growing up knew me as "Cookie" and could only see me through that youthful lens.

It wasn't until I started moving in professional circles that I felt impressed to tell them to refrain calling me by that name. I had entered a new season of life, one that required me to grow up, to align myself with who God called me to be—an influencer. I needed a name, my name, the gift given to me at birth that would speak to and point me in the direction of my God-given destiny. "Cookie," the person was suitable for the early years of my life, but she had evolved into a woman ready to find her place in the world.

I maintain relationships with those that knew me growing up. However, I've redefined those relationships by redefining what I allow them to call me. Some have complied, and some have not. If we are out on a public platform and someone who knew me back "when" would address me as "Cookie," I would stop them and say, "My name is Wanda." Some were offended by my redirection, but it was necessary as I would not allow a childhood perception or my past to take the journey with me into my future.

I am in no way insisting that women bearing the name "Cookie" cannot be successful in life or business; they can. I'm simply sharing my journey because the name attached to my childhood often kept people engaging with me from that perspective, and that had to change. For me, it had become bigger than the name itself. It was about the perception and image I was growing out of and the woman I matured to become.

At the time of this writing, as the Coronavirus, better known as the COVID-19 pandemic, is ravishing nations, a couple in India gave birth to newborn twins naming them Corona and Covid. Perhaps the parents sought to acknowledge the current state of the world at the time of their birth. The names of their children, however, will forever be associated with the death of hundreds of thousands of people.

Take time; find out what your name means.

Take time; find out what your name means. If you discover positive qualities and attributes, live up to them. If there are negative connotations or meanings associated with your name and your life is reflective of that negativity, change it. You have the power to redefine your name by the life you chose to live.

I attribute the influence of my life to Proverbs 22:1 as a foundation. While I understand the perspective, some assume of not caring what others think of them; a mature person understands that a good name does matter. You need to be mindful of who you are perceived to be. You cannot change how people perceive you, but you can give them the truth of who you are. If they develop a negative perception, let it be what they created and not what you've displayed before them.

I execute business with the focal point that my name is invaluable, and everything attached to the name Wanda must reveal a heart of integrity. Integrity is doing things right, because it's right, and doing it the right way. Your heart reveals your motives. Pure motives ensure an easier resolution even if things don't go as planned or if challenges arise.

I Am Not for Sale.

Don't sell yourself short; a good character cannot be bought. Being bought has many connotations and can show up in various ways. You should not sacrifice or sell your name for a seat, position, or place in a relationship. Your name is the most valuable commodity you will ever own. Steward it well. Never abuse or misuse it.

There are examples throughout history and across the world where people have chosen riches, favor, and even alliances over a good name. Often the outcomes of their choice include corruption, bad business dealings, and nations in poverty. In times gone by, I've been asked to attach my name to business ventures that did not necessarily reflect my heart or character. Therefore, the use of my name was not an option.

When you hold positions of influence and power, people will pursue your name for endorsements, at times, creating a challenge. Don't be quick to give a "yes" until your understanding is sure. You want to be sure they are just as committed to having a good name and walking in integrity as you are. Know if a person is seeking an endorsement because they have a personal agenda aimed at accessing your network or your platform. Alliances based on access and not on an aligning cause or mission are destined to fail. I've declined to give and receive several endorsements when it was clear an individual was more interested in my platform than advancing my cause. My cause will always be aimed toward the betterment of others.

Refuse to be sold. Do not allow position, recognition, or an opportunity to auction you off to the highest bidder. It's never worth it.

A Good Name Produces Influence and Develops Your Legacy.

When your name is good, your influence is respected. I don't need the highest paid or the most prestigious position. My circle of influence has taken me to places I know I couldn't have gotten to on my own. I've been given positions of authority because of the confidence my name holds. In my current career, I report to the executive vice president, but I am not a vice president. However, my position has the influence of one. Influence is more than a position. It is not something to be bragged on or flaunted, but instead modeled and honored.

My great grandfather Lewis Cherry was a man of great stature and character. At six feet tall, he was a hospitable, cordial man, and he never met a stranger. He died when I was in my twenties, but my legacy of influence began with him. I recall the early days of my childhood traveling down south; the community knew who I was because they knew who he was. His children, grandchildren, and even great-grandchildren were expected to display excellent manners and respect at all times.

Our family is rich in heritage and community, which produces a wealth that is often hard to find. One way we celebrate this wealth is by connecting monthly for what we call "Family Day." This day is about honoring one another while celebrating the gift of family.

I look forward to this cross-generation gathering with my family. We share laughter, exchange recipes, play games, and strengthen our bond with each other. Friends are invited because not everyone is blessed with a biological family that connects. I understand it may be challenging for people to stay connected to their lineage because relationships in families can be fragmented.

> *We make it our intention to uphold our core value of living in integrity.*

I realize some may not know much about their family lineage. However, I believe there is no better way to discover your history and hear the stories that have shaped your family legacy than by coming together. If you are fortunate enough to identify your family lineage, do all you can to stay connected to it. If it does not represent the legacy you want to reflect, then become the foundation of something better.

The people in my family haven't been perfect. However, the names are good and will be carried on, remembered generation after generation. While my family has flaws, we make it our intention to uphold our core value of living in integrity. From Cherry to Davis, Davis to Gray, and Gray to Montgomery, there is a thread of integrity woven throughout my lineage, of which we are proud and unashamed.

My mother made sure the Gray family name would be a pillar in our community. The Grays are known for having faith in God, generous giving, and a family business in childcare. My mother served as the founder and director of one of the largest childcare centers in our city. She consistently modeled the power of giving and serving others. I watched her give everything she had, ensuring the business thrived while at the same time positively impacting the community. The business carried our name and therefore had to, without question, reflect our integrity and values. Everyone connected to the business understood this and dedicated themselves to upholding this commitment.

Not many know this, but there were times my mother wouldn't take a salary so the business would survive. I recall years of her writing off debt for individuals because she knew they could not afford the extra expense of childcare. There are families standing today because of the support my mother graciously gave them. Young mothers who needed care for their young children, while finishing school, are now successful businesswomen who remember the Gray family name. The impact your family has on other families will never be forgotten.

Legacy is not just about your lineage; it is also about your impact on the community around you, and it's the mark you leave on the world.

My Mother Taught Me Well.

My great-grandfather taught me the importance of legacy and influence, but my mother taught me the importance of having a trusted name. The lessons weren't formal, but she gave me responsibilities not given to my older sister. Those responsibilities established her confidence in my name and my abilities. My mother trained me to be trustworthy by assigning tasks within the family, like going to the store or helping care for my siblings. I could be counted on.

There was never a question as to if I would do it. I just did it—my obedience and ability to follow instructions developed a relationship of trust between us. My mother knew I would do what I was told to do how I was told to do it, and when I was told to do it. No questions asked. Through those experiences, I learned that I was a leader.

I grew up on Eighth and Sommers in the Hillside Projects. My parents had children just about every year, 1953, 1954, 1956, 1957, 1958, 1960, 1961, 1963, and 1972. We also have a plus one, which is a sister we adopted as a part of our family. Coming from a big family, you learned to play and get along with each other. Three boys followed my birth, so naturally, I played with the boys. By the time my younger sisters came along, I spent enough time playing with the boys that I didn't like all the things the girls did. I wasn't interested in playing house or playing with dolls; I was more of what is called a tomboy.

There were always so many children around between the neighborhood children and us. Even though I was a child, I was looked at as the leader and the responsible one among us. My presence exuded responsibility. I'm not the oldest child in my family, and I wasn't the oldest child in the neighborhood, but I was often treated like it. My natural instinct to lead was evident even as a child. If the gift of leadership is inside you and a need for leadership around you—rise to the occasion.

Each time I rose to the opportunity of leadership, it increased trust in my name. Don't shrink or minimize who you are to fit into a space you think you're supposed to be. If you are the answer to a need, respond.

Protect Your Name.

You protect your name by living a life so that when people hear it, it can be easily deciphered if the circumstances of discussion are reflective of you, or them. Your life should live up to your name, and your name should live up to your life. I've been in situations where my name has come up, and others in the room knew the content being discussed wasn't true because they knew my name. They knew the value of my name, and they knew the life that I lived associated with my name. Very similarly, there have been situations of advocacy where my name has come up, and right away, there is a connection between my name, my life, my character, and the situation at hand.

> *Protecting your name is greater than you; it is for your legacy.*

Eliminate any confusion around who you are and what your name represents. If they are the same, people should know within the first five seconds of your name entering an arena if the discussion at hand is true or false. Your name speaks in rooms that you aren't in; because of this, it's vital that when you are in places your voice, your words, your name, and your character all line-up. You protect your name by doing right; don't do wrong.

I've encountered others where confusion and distortion surround who they claim to be and who they are, to the point that when they show up, it cheapens the credibility of their name.

Protecting your name is greater than you; it is for your legacy. Growing up, my grandfather was an important part of our family because our father had a drinking problem. What we would treat now as an alcohol and other drug abuse disorder, we called a drinking problem back then. Based on my father's behavior, he would have fit the conditions of AUD or alcohol use disorder. AUD categorized as a chronic relapsing brain disease by the National Institute on Alcohol and Abuse.

His disorder caused him to be in and out of the home on occasion, and when he was away, my grandfather stepped in. Having a good name in your family doesn't mean that your family is perfect. Good and perfect are not the same thing. When your name is good, you strive to do good. You try to live up to who you say you are. You do right by people, and that makes your name good. I haven't found a perfect family just yet. If you do, let me know.

What I'll say about my father is that there were things he did that weren't perfect, but it didn't stop my family from having a good name.

Our grandfather protected the legacy of our name each time he stepped in during the absence of my father. He was the pastor of New True Light Baptist church on 12th and Garfield. I remember going to church with my grandparents. It's easy for me to stay connected to my faith because faith has always been a part of my life. It was modeled generations before me. Some of the best memories about going to my grandfather's church are the times we had breakfast at their house. It was always the same, bacon, eggs, toast, and grape jelly.

I can easily recall the memories of my siblings and I having breakfast while my grandparents prepared for service. Now that I am a grandmother, I value the time I have with my grandchildren. I model before them what it means to have a good name. I want them to know the importance of not only our family name but of their individual names. I want their names to be good. Just as I did with their parents, I am teaching them the value of a good name and protecting it.

My son runs a business, and someone reached out to me to tell me what a good job he's doing. They shared with me that when working with him, they always know what kind of service they're going to get. My son strives to provide excellent service, just as he should. I raised him to make sure the services he offers leave a good reputation behind his name. When I am out in the community, and someone approaches me about my children, I expect to hear good things because I know they understand the value of their name.

Your Name Travels with You.

Throughout life, you will have job transitions; you may move to a new neighborhood or attend a new church or social club. No matter where you go, your name goes with you. You don't get to pick up and leave your name behind. It's attached to you forever. For some people, they aren't able to stay connected to things or people too long because they have given themselves a bad name.

Any transition you experience, you want to do it in a way that people are glad you were there and miss you when you are gone. Your name creates an experience that people remember forever. A good name is chosen, which means you can decide what people will experience through your name. The experience others have with you must be authentic. Strive to ensure it leaves a lasting imprint and life impact.

The Will To Do

Free yourself of this excuse:
"I cannot accomplish anything because what other folks have put me through"
Activate your brilliant mind and take off your blinders.
The Will To Do is within you.
Poverty may have been a constant companion, segregation, discrimination, and back seats, too. Nevertheless, it's time to rid yourself
Of all the baggage and break the cycle.
Because,
The Will To Do is within you.

By: Bessie Gray

Chapter Two

Be Authentic
Maintain your confidence and do not conform.

"And be not conformed to this world: but be ye transformed by the renewing of your mind, that ye may prove what is that good and acceptable, and perfect, will of God." - Romans 12:2 (KJV)

I believe my life experiences can help someone. Young women are constantly asking to sit with me and have the chance to "pick my brain." My persona of influence graces me the opportunity to connect with young women who are trailblazers in their own right. I value these moments because I understand how important they were for me as a young woman developing into the leader I am today.

I have been told I am a template for being a woman of faith and a professional in corporate arenas and social settings.

Women in the professional setting want to sit with me because they are curious as to how I've attained the positions I've had while maintaining my faith. The first thing I tell them is that no one can make you do anything you don't want to do.

You don't have to assimilate or conform to behaviors that are not representative of your faith or God. I don't conform because I don't have too. My mind is transformed. I don't drink. I don't smoke. I can also go out with others who are drinking and smoking and not be impacted or bothered by their choices because I know who I am. Can I drink? Can I smoke? If I want to, but I don't. It's not who I am.

When I see women my age, and they are not living to their fullest potential, I wonder how different our lives must have been to end up so dissimilar. I know that it comes down to choices, both the choices we've made and the choices we continue to make. It's never too late to do something meaningful with the life you've created for yourself. I'm 65, retiring, or what I like to call "repurposing," and I feel good about it. My lifestyle was different because it was my choice. I didn't go out and party and smoke. I didn't do alcohol and drugs then, and I don't do them now. I am aware that there are people my age that still engage in activities that are detrimental to their health and their life. You choose your path to authenticity, and this guides your life.

Commit to living authentically with confidence.

Even as a young woman, I was committed to staying true to who I was. One of the challenges I see most young women have in staying true to who they are is the fact that they don't know who they are. If you cannot clearly say this is who I am, this is what I will do, what I won't do, and what I want out of life, you need to take time to find out who you are.

You cannot be authentic to something you have not defined. When I talk to young women, I encourage them to be consistent in who they are so that people know who to expect. In a time where it is easy to become consumed by social media and by what current culture says you should be, it is an intentional choice not to conform to things that do not represent the values you intend to uphold.

Maintaining my confidence and refusing to conform were values I embraced as a girl. In elementary school, we were avid churchgoers, so I grew up with a strong faith and a moral compass. I don't take my upbringing for granted because I know so many families that lack that foundation.

We were what they called "pew babies," attending church on Sunday morning, Sunday evening, Wednesday night, and Friday night. I remember sleeping on the pews with my siblings during some of the evening services.  We may have been sleeping, but we were there. My family did not have a car, so one of the members would pick us up, and we would be piled into the car with no seatbelts and sitting on each other's laps.

You cannot be authentic to something you have not defined.

The mental image of that makes me laugh and would be something utterly illegal today, but it's how we got around back then. The church mothers, who were seasoned women of influence, were instrumental in our lives. They were role models for us and were extended maternal figures, hence the title "church mothers." We played with their children and spent time at their house and vice versa. My mother was never concerned that we would get around other children or other families and misbehave. She knew we would do what she had taught us to do.

As a big sister, I had no problem reminding my siblings who we were and how we were to behave and conduct ourselves. There was a time to play and have fun, and then there was a time to do the things we were supposed to do. I was committed to making sure we acted accordingly whether our mom was around or not. People didn't mind allowing us to ride with them or inviting us over because we knew how to behave. While our family had structure, we were still allowed to be children and do things like play outside, run around, participate in sports, and enjoy the life of a child.

When life happens, prayer works.

Our background of faith was strict and immersed in prayer and the Word of God. A series of events in my childhood taught me dependence on God and produced the life of prayer that I have to this day. I know that when situations happen, God is present; He knows exactly what's going on. Prayers from church spilled over into all areas of our lives.

I remember playing with my brothers one day, and one of them pushed me off the monkey bars cracking one of my front teeth. I recall another incident where I was playing with a friend by one of the doors in our housing unit. I was on the inside, while my friend was on the outside, and we were both pushing the door. Before we knew it, my hand went through the glass. I cut my thumb and wrist and needed eight stitches. I still have a visible scar from this accident. These things taught me that sometimes when you are playing, accidents happen. It also showed me that God was present through the comfort I felt at those moments, and my first inclination to pray.

Childhood accidents or things that happened to me and incidents, things that happen around me, were one of the many ways my relationship with God grew through prayer. Making prayer, my first response in any situation, proved to be vitally important. The power of prayer was evident again when two families who lived in the Hillside Projects with us got into a terrible car accident. A teenager, a little older than I was died. Another teenager was seriously injured.

Around the same time, a cousin, who was a year or two younger than I, was killed while crossing the street. They lived near us, and while on her way to school, a car struck her. She was the oldest of her siblings and we shared some of the same responsibilities as older children. Her funeral was the first funeral I attended, and it was devastating for me. As a child, I did not fully understand what death meant. However, my life was so rooted in prayer, that despite these tragedies, I remained confident God was with me.

Learning of God's presence even in death at an early age would comfort me later in my life. Prayer doesn't mean that things go your way; prayer is your connection with God that secures you even when they don't. Unfavorable incidents may still befall you, and bad things may happen; however, prayer transcends circumstances in your life. Prayer has been my source of peace and the foundation of my relationship with God. People may look at you and assume that you have everything together and that your life is perfect, but God knows what you've seen and what you've experienced. He knows about every accident and incident. I trusted God through prayer then, and I trust Him now.

Prayer transcends circumstances in your life...

Who you are did not begin today.

Knowing who I am has come as a result of knowing who God says I am. God has made me secure in my identity. I'm not looking for somebody to tell me who I am or to affirm who I am. Nor am I looking for anybody to tell me who God is or to affirm who He is to me. I already know.

The foundation of who I am today started years ago. I learned organizational skills from helping my mom keep things organized in the house for my siblings and me. Although I wasn't the oldest, my mother would give me the responsibility to lead. If she sent us to the store, she would give me the list and the money, and my sister would come along. I would make sure we had everything on the list, paid exactly what we were supposed to, and got all of our change back. I would double-check the list, read it out loud, and check our cart to make sure everything was there.

We would finish our shopping and then use what we now call an Uber or Lyft to get home. Before ride-sharing services existed, there were trusted black men in the community who offered rides home from the grocery store. My mother confirmed that these men were safe, and they would give us a ride back home with the groceries. We knew who they were, and they knew who we were. My mother never had to worry about us trying anything or acting out of character because she could trust us. She could also trust the men to bring us straight home and make sure we were safe.

I remember going shopping with my mother and sister at the department store called Gimbles. My sister needed to go to the bathroom. The clerk showed us how to get to the elevator. Back then, people operated the elevators. Once we went to the bathroom, we went back to the elevator to find our mother. The operator tried to take us somewhere else. My antennas went up right away and I knew something was wrong.

Nobody had ever told me that if something happens to you or if somebody tries to take you somewhere, make sure you scream, I just knew that was the right thing to do. I remember screaming and calling for my mother, and somehow, we were able to get reconnected with her. There was no way I would allow my sister and me to end up where we weren't supposed to be, and I made sure everyone in the store knew it.

Through this experience, I found my voice. I learned to use my voice and advocate for myself and others. My early years revealed there was something unique about me. I also learned that my faith and focus on God needed to be unwavering.

You always have a choice.

When people talk to me about the different things they've encountered, I often talk to them about choices. For example, I've counseled people who are challenged in their relationships with others and in taking ownership of how they respond. After hearing their concerns, I ask how they reacted to the situation and how that response influenced the outcome.

While you cannot control everything, you can make decisions about your behavior and how you respond. I am who I am because of the choices I've made. Live life from a decision-based perspective. In my life, I've made the best choices, given what God has allowed.

My sister and I were among the first students to desegregate Samuel Morse Middle School in Milwaukee, Wisconsin. Education disparities were rampant in the '60s. In schools designated for "colored" only, resources were inadequate, and learning gaps between black and white students were evident. Even attending the best "colored" schools did not offer the education racially integrated schools provided.

I took the possibility of a quality education seriously. Developments in the education system allowed additional opportunities for learning that I pursued. Working hard and taking extra classes landed me a year ahead, placing me in the same grade as my older sister. She was not happy about it.

There are some things we will do in life and some places we will end up that will not make others happy. It is not your responsibility to control the happiness of another. My advancement highlighted challenges already existing between my sister and me. However, being placed in a situation where the odds were against us, fortified the bond between us. We had to leave the house around 6:30 am to ride the city bus for nearly an hour to make it to school on time.

Integrating into an all-white school was not easy. The racial inequalities and struggles of the time were real, and we were in the line of fire every day. It was common to be called inappropriate names and have our white peers attempt to bully us for being at "their" school. Some of the "colored" students responded by fighting and were asked to leave the school because of their behavior. Others did not give the learning experience a chance because the verbal and sometimes physical attacks were unbearable. Both my sister and I, however, weathered the challenges and graduated moving on to attend Lincoln High School.

Life is a series of choices...

Fighting was an option for me as well, but it was not a choice I made because I had already learned to use my voice. I coupled this with confidence and owned the success I was destined to achieve. I refused to allow what was happening around me in terms of racism and unfair treatment to dictate my future. They could not dictate something I owned.

Little did I know, 40 years down the road, I would find myself confidently using my voice again in the face of inequality and adversity. The discipline I developed during high school equipped me for some of the most significant accomplishments of my lifetime. Life is a series of choices. Throughout mine, I've decided to own my responses to what happens around me.

Know who you are.

When you don't know who you are and you aren't living authentically, you make it possible for others to dictate your future. There were times while integrating into a new school, I could have responded to some of the unfairness. However, I knew I had to decide if it was worth it or not. Often, it wasn't.

You must know when to transfer your energy. I often say, "don't get down in the mess." Some moments required me to respond, but once I said what needed to be said, I moved on. I was not stuck in the moment because the experience did not define me—I knew who I was. Lacking clarity in who you are leaves room for experiences to define you.

Knowing who I am and living a life reflective of that knowledge has kept me out of a lot of situations, ongoing disputes, and battles. I don't get involved in the messy stuff because I'm not messy. No matter what happens, you must be consistent in who you are. Whether I was participating in a church event where I knew I was loved and supported, or if I was participating in a school event where I knew I could be discriminated against and treated unfairly, it didn't matter. I was going to be who I knew I was; my identity was consistent.

I watched people around me conform and try to fit in. I wondered how hard that must be, to try and be something you're not. I refused to put effort into being somebody else because being me was enough.

Over time, my faith in God, belief in prayer, and the power of my voice developed and matured. There are some things I know about myself, and there are no questions about it. I don't have to blink or even think about it because I know me. When you are that confident in who you are conforming to anything or anybody else isn't a struggle because you have no desire to be a copy.

Chapter Three

Invest in Relationships
Remain loyal and manage your expectations

"Give, and it shall be given unto you; good measure, pressed down, and shaken together, and running over, shall men give into your bosom. For with the same measure that ye meet withal it shall be measured to you again." - Luke 6:38 (KJV)

Relationships matter. While often attributed to finances, I want to reflect on this verse in correlation with relationships. When you make meaningful investments in others, you may see a relational return that surpasses financial gain.

The treasure I've been able to obtain through people I've met in my life is immeasurable. Experience has revealed to me that relationships are essential. Connecting with others is a value I hold at the very core of my being.

People often make assumptions about who we are before meeting us. They've heard of us or experienced us through someone else's perspective and determine they know us. In this regard, we are known by more people than we think.

Social media has made this even more prominent. Take note that your social media image and profile clearly represent who you are. Your physical presence and online presence should be parallel and reflect a healthy balance. When people follow you or become your friend, they believe they know you. However, this type of introduction is only a summary of who you portray to be.

People are also introduced to us by others who know us. Coming from a big family, some people know me because of my siblings. However, they don't actually know me.

Why is this important? People perceive who you are, even if they have never met you. Because of this, you must protect your reputation through the relationships you build. Make sure you are proud of the experiences you have with others and maintain meaningful connections.

Relationships in your past can impact your future.

I've attended the same church, maintained positive relationships with high school friends, and former neighbors for more than 40 years. Significant accomplishments in my life have been established on the foundation of those relationships. There have been moments of disagreement, but it doesn't matter, I still build on them. You never know when you will need a relationship.

All relationships bring value, even the ones that aren't the best can teach you what not to do. I've seen relationships go different ways yet come back full circle.

When I look at my life now and what I'm doing as the Village President of Brown Deer, Wisconsin, people tell me I was doing this in high school. Those that know me have said I've always been a leader and organizer. Some of it I remember, some of it I listen to and enjoy their memories. Their current perspective is based on the relationships I had with them at the time.

I've learned you may come across the same people over and over again, so be careful how you engage with others. Don't dismiss anyone. I genuinely believe the person that's the secretary today could be the president tomorrow. That's how life works.

Controlling yourself and maintaining your integrity is a choice.

I recognize where I am now has been in the making through the relationships I've formed with others. People think that I have charted my course to this point, but I have not. Having integrity, honoring commitments, and being professional will open doors you desire to enter.

Obliging a changing social culture that devalues relationships, having a foul mouth, and being loud, may seem trendy. However, it can also abort the course you desire to take.

It's easy to get upset and fly off the handle; controlling yourself and maintaining your integrity is a choice. I encounter so many young people who say, "It's just the way I am." I want them to know they can choose to be something different. Putting words together to cuss somebody out is not a skill set, and really, how far does that get you? You've cussed them out, now what? You've tarnished the relationship, and something that could have been a resource for you is now gone.

My first unofficial job came through a resource that was built upon a relationship. My high school homeroom teacher needed a babysitter. She watched how I carried myself and the way I interacted with my peers and teachers—so she offered me an opportunity to work for her. She and I are still friends to this day.

She supported my campaign for Village President by collecting signatures, promoting the campaign among her neighbors, and providing monetary support. If you know anything about running a campaign, you know you need people who support and believe in you. You need relationships.

My first official job was as a summer camp counselor for Northcott Neighborhood Center. As a teenager, I assisted an adult staff member, and we were responsible for leading activities for younger children. We would take the bus to the park, stay all day and then return to the center.

My second job was a 10-key proof operator for a bank when I was in the 12th grade. I participated in the Office Education Program, which provided students with hands-on experience in real-life jobs.

This program gave me skills that prepared me for the professional world, and I still maintain relationships with some of the people I met during that time. I believe opportunities like this are valuable for young people, and I support and advocate for them as often as I can.

Relationships can be the key to opportunities.

Throughout my professional journey, the positions I've held did not come by way of being a traditional interviewee. Instead, my interview process has been through reputable relationships. When you meet people and establish a good relationship with them, they remember you when opportunities become available. At almost every place I've worked, the offer came because someone invited me to apply or recommended me for the position. My career path has been non-conventional because of relationships.

A career defining role I held was through a large social service agency. They received a contract that extended its services from the south side of the city to the north side of the city. A service extension meant exponential growth and was a big deal at the time. The vice president of the organization, and I had met years earlier through a consulting relationship. After I finished the services for him, we remained in communication.

When the agency experienced growth, he contacted me. He said he was looking for a strong manager to run the north side office. I did not have the background in the services they offered; however, he insisted we meet. I explained to him I'd never done that type of work, but he said it didn't matter. He needed a strong manager, and that is what he saw in me.

When people have a need, they will think of whom they know that can meet that need. You may not be knowledgeable in a particular area. Yet, if you have other strengths, relationships will put you in positions you otherwise would not be able to obtain.

The vice president invited me for an interview. Afterward, the president flew in from Virginia to meet with me as well. I was hired and became responsible for the start-up, onboarding staff, and managing the northside office. I was successful in that position, and while I was there, I continued to build relationships. One of the relationships I developed was with Making Connections Milwaukee.

At the time, Milwaukee was considered one of the worst places in the country for black people. Economic disparity and micro-inequities impacted hot spots in the city, and this initiative provided wrap-around community services in hard-hit areas. I was honored to join the mission, and my influence continued to grow through relationships.

Not long after that, an invitation came to apply for a position at Children's Family and Community Partnerships as executive director. This organization was a subsidiary of Children's Hospital of Wisconsin. When considering this opportunity, once again, I did not have a specific background in child welfare. Still, I had other strengths and connections that made me a perfect fit for the position.

Within four years of being in this role, I took on a special project. There was a shortage of foster care families across the city, and our goal was to increase those numbers. Historically, this project had a net gain of about 35 families per project cycle. When they invited me in, I pulled all of my resources together and created a team for the project. I petitioned churches, businesses, sororities, radio and television stations, community groups, and any place that allowed me to share the critical need for foster care families. We produced a net gain of over 130 families, nearly 4x previous outcomes. People asked how I accomplished the task; the answer was simple – relationships.

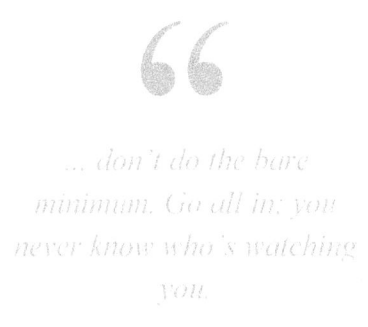

... don't do the bare minimum. Go all in; you never know who's watching you.

When people invite you to work on a team or to complete a project, don't do the bare minimum. Go all in; you never know who's watching you. The success of this project caused executive leadership at Children's Hospital to take note.

Recently appointed, the executive vice president who had just relocated to Milwaukee from Tennessee asked me if I wanted to join his team. The connections I developed through Children's Family and

Community Partnerships were impressive, and Children's Hospital desired to expand their direct community impact as well.

They noticed the relationships I had in the community and the way people responded to me. The executive vice president shared there was a template for the job description, and they could go out and hire someone. However, he noted that I was already doing the work. I was allowed to support the further development of the newly created job description and transition from the role I was in to become the director of community partnerships for Children's Hospital. This position has been one of the most fulfilling opportunities in my professional career. It has been an honor serving in this role, and it is the perfect transition to retire into my life's work of community service and meaningful connections with others.

Sow seeds that produce a bountiful relational harvest.

Professionally and personally, I've seen a harvest from the relationship seeds I've sown. Personally, the relationship with my husband, Floyd, has given us both the gift of our children and 47 years of marriage. I met my husband in college, and we had our first date on my birthday, November 17th. He took me to see *The Valachi Papers*, which was released on November 3, 1972, starring Charles Bronson. The memories are so clear; I can almost smell the popcorn.

People have inquired about sustaining a marriage of 47 years, and what makes it successful. I'll be the first to admit that 47 years of marriage did not come easy. My husband has never been abusive, and we don't fight, however, even a seemingly perfect marriage is work. We've committed to each other to invest in our relationship. A commitment means you're in it for the long haul and not just when things are good. He hasn't always been right, and I haven't always been right either. Neither of us is perfect. If perfection were grounds for a successful marriage, all marriages would dissolve.

All marriages have challenges, and I have been a confidant for others when issues arise. I listen from a place of understanding and never a position of judgment. After hearing whatever has transpired, I always desire to learn what each person's role was in the situation. I am an advocate for marriage and often remind others, "you won't reap the benefits of relationships if you keep quitting."

I know people that have been married three or four times, and they have missed the benefits because they viewed marriage as a contract to be broken and not as a commitment to be kept. There are times an opportunity may present itself to walk away from your marriage. Staying committed in relationships is a choice. Commitments are more comfortable to keep when you've done your due diligence in selecting a mate.

For example, if you value education, your mate should be academically astute. If you identify early in the relationship that they are not, reconsider your choice. Demonstrating a lack of mastery for the English language or the inability to spell should be a deal-breaker for you. People will show you signs that they are not a good fit and sometimes, we overlook those signs. I encourage you to pay attention to signs and indicators if a romantic relationship does not mirror what you desire in a mate. I have yet to understand why people make commitments when they have no desire to invest in staying committed.

I was confident I wanted to invest in a relationship with Floyd. Before Floyd, I dated another guy, but he did not elicit a desire in me to offer my commitment. Floyd seemed like an abrupt change, and not everyone understood it, but I did. I knew what I was willing to commit to and what I could

It's essential to manage your expectations.

not. Floyd won my heart and my desire to commit. It's essential to manage your expectations. If someone comes to you a certain way and they're already displaying to you who they are, don't marry them, hire them, or invite them to be your friend with the expectation of changing them. That's not fair to them or you.

You don't order something from a restaurant, get it to the table, and then tell the chef you expected something else. They would probably ask you to leave the restaurant or try to find out what you did not understand about the menu.

What you plant in your family will grow in your legacy.

When Floyd and I started dating, I knew he was the right fit for me, and that I could be committed to him. In the middle of a snowstorm in April of 1973, Floyd asked me to marry him. We were married in August of that same year. We met, dated, got engaged, and married all within nine months. We started our family the next year, requiring me to make some changes like withdrawing from college to focus on raising a family.

Raising our family was important to me. I wanted to be there for my children. I wanted to be involved in their school life and make sure they had hot meals. I wanted them to know the stability of a home with a mother and father. One of the non-negotiables while raising our children was an evening family dinner. I always cooked and made sure we had time to sit down together for dinner. It is during these times I learned about my children. I would listen to them share their hearts about what was going on in their lives. The seeds of love sown at the dinner table developed a bond that matured through their adolescence and into adulthood.

We were given the gift to share this bond with our community through our local newspaper, The Milwaukee Journal. The paper was doing an article highlighting families and the importance of family dinner. When the opportunity arose, I didn't have to create a family dinner experience; we already had one. We simply displayed for the local paper what we did in our home every day.

It blesses me to know that my children now carry this tradition within their families. Although it looks different in their respective households, they make time for family and to have a meal together. The relationship between our children and us is now modeled between my children and their children. Legacy has been established.

I pray for this legacy, especially in the global unrest of COVID-19, that is happening as I write this book. My eldest grandchildren are seniors in high school, and I'm interested to see how God will use their lives. They have already experienced pivotal moments in their lives facing challenges beyond their control.

Both were born in fall 2001, when our country experienced a terrorist attack that changed life as we knew it and has been forever sealed in history as "9/11." My grandson was born on September 22nd, and my granddaughter was born on October 5th. The terrorist attack on September 11th was a difficult time in America. I remember sitting and watching the morning news when it flashed that a plane had crashed into the twin towers in New York City.

I had already purchased plane tickets to Boston when the attacks happened. I was set to leave on September 20th to be with my daughter for the birth of her son. I cherish the relationships that I have with my children, and it was important for me to be there for her during this time. People started asking me if I was afraid or if I would still fly to be with her. It was a no brainer for me, of course, I would. That's my daughter, and she was having my grandson.

I arrived in Boston on September 20th, and my grandson was born on the 22nd. I would not have missed that moment for anything. No terror could keep me away from witnessing my daughter experience the miracle of motherhood. I stayed for a week and then returned home.

After returning home, I had a business trip planned two weeks later. I was leaving with several of my colleagues, and on October 4th, I received a call that my daughter-in-law was in labor. During pivotal moments in our children's lives, we've made a point to have at least one parent present. Floyd was there for our granddaughter's birth on October 5th.

Now, in the middle of a global pandemic, both of my grandchildren are seniors in high school. They are living in an unprecedented time that will leave a lasting impression on their lives. Due to the pandemic, they won't be able to walk across the stage and experience traditional graduation. As a family, we are planning a graduation parade to celebrate their accomplishments. Both my granddaughter and grandson have been accepted to Syracuse University in New York. They plan to attend in the Fall of 2020. I am proud of their achievements and their resilience.

As they prepare to begin college life, they will experience a new reality, much like the global dynamics that shifted the year they were born. They will need to lean on the relationships around them, with their parents, grandparents, friends, and community. They must adapt to a college transition no other high school class has experienced in their lifetime.

Everything they expected and even our hopes to celebrate this monumental moment in their life has shifted. Life, as we know it, must be modified in response to the global pandemic. During the writing of this book, most of the country has been under a "safer at home order." Meaning, we are strongly discouraged from gathering with others outside our home. Public gatherings are restricted to no more than ten people, and everyone is encouraged to wear facial masks to prevent the transmission of the disease. COVID-19 has introduced a new term into our way of living called "social distancing" - requiring those in the same space to maintain a distance of at least 6 ft between each other.

The invitations purchased for their traditional graduation won't go out because the graduation events have been canceled. I am thankful they both took full advantage of their high school experience and attended prom in their junior year. Missing the high school prom experience is one disappointment they have circumvented.

A month before their scheduled graduation, my mother, their great grandmother, turned 86. Her birthday gave us a chance to practice a large family gathering, virtually. Over 90 family members and friends joined us online to celebrate through Zoom, a video streaming platform. Virtual meetings and video conferencing platforms have become a common way for people to stay connected while social distancing. There is power in connection and community. People joined us from all over the country, including California, Arizona, Texas, Florida, New York, New Hampshire, Wisconsin, Washington D.C., and more.

It was a beautiful display of love and celebration, one that we will recreate for my grandchildren to honor their passage from high school to college. As a family, we are creative. Our celebration may look different than what we all hoped, but it will be full of family and full of love.

> There is power in connection and community.

Relationships are not easy, but they are worth it.

Relationships may require sacrifice. While not easy, when we understand the value of relationships, it's worth it. I have given up what I want for the relationships I value. When I determine a sacrifice is needed, I consult God first. I trust His guidance on managing relationships. The concept of sacrifice can seem overwhelming; however, sometimes, it is simply positioning yourself to be a solution to a problem. Those in a relationship with me can count on me to be solution-oriented. I'm a reliable resource. If we need to figure it out, I'm here to help.

There are times I have been called on to figure out challenging situations that involved litigation affecting our family and extended family. I stood up as our family representative to face the backlash that was coming against us. My voice of advocacy was for due process for those in my family. Not suggesting a position of right or wrong, but due process.

I don't believe in throwing people away because they do something unfavorable or because something unfortunate happened. When you are in a relationship with people, especially family, you help them find solutions. In an esteemed professional role, I was committed to helping someone I love navigate an unfortunate situation.

People explained to me that because of who I was, I was committing professional suicide. They encouraged me to disassociate myself from the situation. However, I refused to pretend that what was happening was not happening and that it did not involve people that I love. You can't have relationships with people only when it looks good for you.

At the time of the situation, I had over 350 team members under me. My approach was, to be honest, share what they needed to know, and then continue being there for my family the way I needed to be. The situation at hand was now public and garnered media attention.

I explained to them the context of what was happening while assuring them the things they may see and hear would not impact them. I refused to turn my back not just on the situation, but on my family. After a year supporting my family member through the litigation, I ended up with a promotion.

When people get in trouble, and you say you're their friend, you don't abandon them. Stay there and remain consistent. People know this about me, and I've heard people say, "if you're in trouble, you need a Wanda on your side." I'm proud of that.

I honor the relationships I've built and all the experiences that have come with them, good and bad.

Chapter Four

Embrace Opportunities
Learn from peaks and valleys and use them to grow.

"Therefore, my beloved brethren, be ye steadfast, unmovable, always abounding in the work of the Lord, forasmuch as ye know that your labor is not in vain in the Lord." 1 Corinthians 15:58 (KJV)

Everything you experience can be an opportunity to grow. Peaks and valleys are learning occasions to glean from along the way. When people see who you are today, they often overlook the path you've taken to where you are now and the experiences you've had to overcome. Valleys evoke feelings of desolation and can be some of the most challenging times in our lives. There are, however, pivotal lessons that only the valley can teach.

A peak is the apex of experience. It is when we are at our best or should be experiencing the height of all things we perceive as good. People tend to have a "peak view" of life, meaning, they can only conceptualize a person at their highest height. However, valley moments are inevitable. It's how you walk in the depth of your valley that determines how high your peaks can go. My peaks and valleys have reaffirmed my truth that life is a series of choices; you have a choice in the outcome. You can choose to accept failure, or you can decide to learn from it. You can get stuck when hard things happen, or you can use them to move you forward.

Faith even in the valley.

I've used the hard things I've experienced in the valleys to grow and trust God more. My mother modeled this for our family by her strong faith in God. We followed her lead and saw the results of her faith manifest through our father's recovery from alcoholism. She was consistent in prayer and love for our father. Somehow she knew that her prayers were not in vain. She believed my dad would recover, and we would be a family again.

It took years, and at times the valleys were low. My mother's demonstration of unwavering faith brought our family through what seemed to be the valley of the shadow of death. I've learned that where shadows exist, there is a light, and among valleys, there are mountain tops.

My father's experience with alcoholism could have been a deterrent for my future. I didn't understand everything that he was going through, but I knew it was not a result of me or anything that I had done. I learned in elementary school that my father was an alcoholic. Again, this was before alcoholism was determined to be an illness, so no one knew that it was something that needed to be treated and not jailed. He struggled a lot and went to jail multiple times. His absence caused our family to often depend on welfare for support.

There were days our dad would come home and was extremely drunk. As a child, it was embarrassing to have your friends witness that type of behavior, but he was our dad, and we loved him. My mother never stopped praying for my dad; she was an example of being steadfast and unmovable.

Do not discount your peak experiences when disheartening moments happen.

As a family of faith, our traditions and beliefs strongly discouraged divorce, so my mother never divorced my father, even after a nine year separation. My dad lived in the same city, but we did not see him much. Although my mother had a husband, she was a single mom during this time. Witnessing her faith walk became the foundation that would take me through one of the lowest valleys in my life.

A peak experience clouded by a valley moment.

It is interesting how some of the highest peaks in our lives can also contain some of the lowest valley moments. Do not discount your peak experiences when disheartening moments happen. I learned this through one of the most significant peaks in my life, my wedding day.

A big wedding wasn't my desire. My mother wanted me to have one because I was the first one to get married. I envisioned a small, intimate wedding, but it grew to a much larger wedding party, including all my sisters except for the youngest. We had five bridesmaids and five groomsmen. That was a big wedding for the seventies.

During this time, my father's condition had improved, and he was no longer drinking. Our family was reunited, and this was priceless to me. I was so excited that at one of the most significant moments in my life, my father was not sick and was able to be present with us. I was looking forward to him giving me away at my wedding. I was counting on it.

With all of the things we had experienced, I wanted to have this moment with him. Little girls dream of their fathers, giving them away at their wedding, and I was no different. Traditionally, the practice of a father giving his daughter away symbolizes the approval of the daughter's chosen mate. The father expects that the groom will take care of his little girl.

I was 18, and the week of our wedding, my father relapsed. I don't know if it was the pressure from planning the wedding or something else, but he started drinking again. If you've ever had experience with someone who struggled with alcoholism, you know that it can go in cycles. It is a disease that affects the proper functioning of the brain. The cycle of addiction is not linear. Sometimes cycles can have days or weeks in between, or they can have months and years in between.

Understanding addiction has helped me accept that the brain becomes dependent on alcohol. I did not understand this then, but I know now. At that moment, for whatever reason, my father felt he needed to drink. He succumbed to the inability to control his physical and emotional dependence. It spoke louder to him than my need for him at the time. As his brain sent him signals, his behavior followed to satisfy the cravings he could not control.

His drinking was devastating to me. It prevented him from supporting in any way. From financial support to his emotional presence, my father was absent.

I've often wondered what the trigger was, but I still don't know. Maybe it was the reality of us growing up and me getting married. Perhaps it was the pressure of having to walk me down the aisle or the financial responsibility. I'm not sure. One thing I am sure of, the week of the wedding, my father lost it. His drinking quickly became out of control, and he spiraled into a dark valley during my peak experience.

Amid the joy of my wedding peak was also the shadow of my father's valley, raising emotions of sadness and anger. I wanted him to pull it together and be there, but he could not. Fitted for his tuxedo, all of the plans were in place, and we were ready for the wedding. It was a moment in my life when I did not know what to do. I didn't know what was going to happen. If you've ever been a bride, you know the stress that goes along with it. Weddings are already a lot to deal with, and for most couples, by the time the date arrives, they just want it all to be over. They are ready to move on with their lives. I know we were.

As much as I wanted the entire experience to be over, we were in a dilemma. My father could not give me away, and we needed to come up with a plan to support him on the day of the wedding because he was drinking so heavily. He could not sober up, and not only was he in no shape to give me away, but he was also in no shape to attend the wedding at all. His drinking was severe.

I needed someone to walk me down the aisle, and I needed somewhere for my father to be as the wedding took place. My two brothers right under me were 17 and 16 years old. My brother, who was 17, had just signed up for the Navy and was away at basic training. He was able to come home, get fitted for a tux, and prepare to give me away.

Now, the task became finding a place for my father. We knew that if my dad were at the wedding, he would disrupt everything because of his drinking. We had to make a difficult choice. I knew my dad was in no shape to participate in the wedding. He was operating under the influence, which meant that he had no control over his impulses, the drinking had consumed him.

On the morning of the wedding, one of my mother's friends came and picked up my dad and drove him out to Waukesha, which was about 45 minutes away from where the wedding would be and dropped him off. She said by the time he figures out how to get back to Milwaukee, the wedding would be over. She was right. The wedding went on with no problem. My brother gave me away, and it was a beautiful day. Now, I can smile at the things we did to make it work; but at the time, it was a hard thing to go through. Most people around me had a "peak view" of our wedding experience, never knowing the valley that tried to overshadow it.

After my dad sobered up and found his way back home, we never talked about what happened.

Leaders lead, even when they grieve.

My dad died ten years ago. I am thankful that before he died, he invited God into his heart and received the gift of salvation. God changed his life and transformed him. He no longer smoked or drank and was committed to my mother and our family.

After receiving a diagnosis of esophageal cancer, his prognosis was 30 days or 6 months. They could not tell us which one it would be. My dad lived for 30 days and passed away on December 3, 2010. Before he died, my siblings who lived out of state and those that lived near spent time with him. I went to the hospital every day to see him.

About a week before he passed, my mother suggested we start talking to a funeral home. She could sense his time was drawing near. As a leader in my family, I knew that by "we," she meant "me." Naturally, the responsibility of planning my father's funeral fell in my lap. My role has always included handling difficult transitions.

The call to lead remains even when leaders experience personal challenges. Losing my father was personal to me; however, I was still a leader.

We knew it would be soon, but we didn't know when. At this time, I was a board member of the National Black Child Development Institute. We had a scheduled meeting in Washington, D.C. Although I was hesitant about going, I kept my plans to participate in the meeting. With a prognosis of 30 days or six months, we were literally at the mercy of time. The reality that I was a daughter losing her father, was something I could not ignore. However, my unction to lead called me away to keep my commitment.

> *My unction to lead called me away to keep my commitment.*

During his final week, I was working on a poem. I wouldn't classify myself as a poet, but I wanted to write something for my dad that reflected what each one of his children meant to him. I had a hard time finishing it. However, when I got on the plane to D.C., God gave me the rest of the words for the poem, and I finished the poem on the flight.

When my plane landed, I noticed missed calls from my sister. I immediately returned her call and learned that our dad was not responding. Right away, I started working on getting an instant flight home. I was willing to pay whatever upcharges there were. I checked with each airline at the airport. I used every resource and measure of advocacy I could to get home. I could not. The only reasonable flight for me to take was the flight I already had scheduled to return home after the meeting.

While I waited to return home, my dad passed away. I got off the plane and headed straight toward the VA hospital. My family and friends were already there waiting. While I was heading to the elevator, one of my friends called to see where I was because they were getting ready to move my father's body out of the room. They kept him in his room so that I could see him.

As I reflect on that moment, I can still feel the devastation. I was overcome with a myriad of emotions, the reality of loss, unanswered questions, and mentally preparing for the next steps. I didn't permit myself to linger in that moment; leadership required me to shift. It was time to plan my father's funeral.

Leaders grieve too. We experience emotions just as intensely; however, we cannot be driven by our feelings when we are trusted to lead. Following the death of my dad, my nephew, who was just 19 years old, died by suicide. Our entire family experienced this valley together, and my heart as a leader was to help us process the unexpected.

My nephew was a bright kid. Everyone who knew him loved him. A recent high school graduate, he had a promising future. One morning, my sister-in-law reached out to me by phone and mentioned he hadn't come home the night before. They were concerned about him because of some other things going on in his life. It was not like him to stay out all night; however, he had recently sustained an injury that impacted his thinking and reasoning.

After speaking with his mom, I prepared for work, and when I arrived, she contacted me again. Her maternal instincts kept her inquiring about his whereabouts. My nephew was her baby boy, and she knew something was wrong. I told her that I would leave work and come to the house to check on her. I wanted to be there with her. When people you love experience valleys, be present with them at that moment.

I was on my way to their house and missed the turn despite knowing the way. I turned on the next street, and there was a stop sign. Ahead of me was a park, and I could see there was a car with a marketing emblem of the company where my nephew worked as a pizza delivery driver. I drove straight ahead, and when I pulled up, I realized that not only was that the emblem of the company my nephew worked for, it was also my nephew's car.

The police were surrounding the vehicle. I got out and explained that the car belongs to my nephew and asked where he was. It was an active scene, and they shared they could not provide me with any information. I explained to them we were looking for him and again asked where he was.

I got back in the car and went around to my sister-in-law's house. A neighbor was approaching their home to tell them that they found a vehicle near the park as she was also aware we were looking for my nephew. I said to her I had just left the park and confirmed that his car was there. When we went inside, my sister-in-law had been watching the news to try and learn of anything going on that might help us discover where my nephew was. It came on the news that they not only found a car, they also found a body.

I drove back to the park, and this time, I went around to the front and found that I could see all the news stations, reporters, and police. I approached one of the officers, and when they asked me who I was, I told them. That's when they confirmed to me they found a body.

My brother was at the Brown Deer police station when he learned of the news. He and my niece drove to the park. My brother wanted to see his son; he wanted to know for sure if that was him. They asked me if I wanted to confirm the body as well and I told them I did not, but I would wait on my brother. I had never seen my brother cry before; it was heartbreaking. His tears hurt my soul. I was determined to do whatever he and his wife needed to get through this unimaginable situation.

I cannot think of a more overwhelming time in our family, especially for my brother, his wife and their other children. No one had an answer to the question of why. Even more complicated, the answer to his whereabouts was not the answer we desired.

Valley's aren't required to come with answers.

There are some valleys in my life where I still have unanswered questions. However, I understand if I were to stay in the valley waiting on the answers to my questions, I would never experience the peaks. The next valley experience I'll share is cherished and dear to my heart. When my husband and I were expecting our third child, we lost our baby.

Women experience miscarriages every day. It can be an overwhelming and indescribable moment, especially when a woman is in her third trimester. I went to the doctor for my check-up, and the doctor noticed that my baby had stopped moving. Before this, we didn't know anything was wrong, but at that appointment, we learned our baby died in my womb.

There was no medical reason why, and they could not provide answers to my questions. I had to be induced and go through labor and delivery. I delivered a baby boy under medical care. Experiencing a miscarriage in the 3rd trimester was one of the most painful personal trials I've ever gone through. It was a valley I had to process as a woman who lost her child while also managing the loss as a wife processing with her husband.

When a woman is pregnant, everyone expects that after nine months or so, there will be a baby. Reasonably so, people had questions. I would run into people, and the first question they would ask is, "what did you have?" In those moments, I felt like I didn't have anything, literally. I had nothing to show for it, and it grieved me to share that our baby died over and over with those who asked.

God doesn't leave us in the valley and only celebrate with us on the peaks.

I had to process things both physically and mentally, including the aftermath of returning home without a baby. In the days leading up to losing my baby, I was nesting. I was fully expecting to bring our son home, and we were prepared for him. Expressing how I felt at the time was hard to do because nobody had any answers to give me. I didn't have words to share how I felt. There were moments I wanted to be left alone, and moments that I didn't want to be alone at all.

I know God was with me both in the times where I needed to be with people and the times where I needed to be by myself. God doesn't leave us in the valley and only celebrate with us on the peaks. He is with us all the time. It doesn't matter how high we climb or how low we sink. He's there. Those things I went through hurt, but as time went on and as God healed my heart, it became easier and easier to handle.

When you experience a valley, you still have to be consistent with who you are. You can't fall apart and become someone you're not because of what you're going through. If you are a person of faith, remain a person of faith in the valley, and a person of faith when things are going well.

Surround yourself with people that can hold you accountable to who you say you are even when times are challenging. Have people that can pray both for you and with you. Prayer and faith have kept me steadfast through every trial and valley I've experienced.

Looking at my life now, I see a beautiful masterpiece, hand-painted by God. Although there are streaks of pain and grief, there are also rays of sunshine and grace.

Deddy's Nine

Felecia was his sidekick
Wanda was his organizer
Percy was his advocate
Bryant was his spiritual advisor
Mark was his barber
Claudia was his cook and housekeeper
Zach was his McDonald's run driver
Tammy was his thrift shopper
LaSonia was his manicurist

WE are all Deddy's kids. Some call him Deddy, some call him pops, but we all called him father.

He called us Poppa, Grandma, do-do, Susie, Hooka, Cookie...

We loved, we laughed, and we lived and enjoyed our Deddy. He has been the laughter in our family and for many others.

We don't know how to say good-bye.
We know that Deddy accepted Christ as his personal Savior, so we say we'll see ya later, in that great getting up morning when those who died in the Lord will get up to meet the Lord in the air. What a great reunion that will be.

By: Wanda Montgomery
To: My Deddy

Chapter Five

Stay the Course
Win or lose; keep going.

"I can do all things through Christ, which strengtheneth me." Philippians 4:13 (KJV)

When quoting this familiar scripture, I often wonder if people really believe it. For me, I am one who genuinely believes I can do all things through Christ. I approach new situations without fear. I have the mindset, "I can do this, and Christ is going to give me the strength to do it."

One example is my experience running for public office. There were many times I could have quit and decided not to run. The opposition was great. Being a woman, and a woman of color already reduced the likelihood that I would win. Not to mention my roots growing up with a family who received public assistance and lived in the Hillside Projects. As our current culture would see it, I was not the ideal candidate.

Facts were, I could not change that I am a woman mature in age, and a person of color; this is the first greeting to those who meet me. While there are some disparities between men and women, blacks and whites, that have progressed, many have not. Sexism, racism, and microaggressions were all factors I encountered directly and indirectly.

As someone who understands the value of relationships, it was vital for me to be out in the community, introducing myself to constituents who had voting power. At one point, while canvassing neighborhoods, the police were called. It was clear that I was a campaigning official. However, a "concerned citizen," as we will call it, made a report that a person was loitering.  It is not uncommon for candidates to get out and meet those in the community they intend to serve. Sometimes this is done by events, canvassing neighborhoods, visiting local businesses, or other activities that connect you with people. Unfortunately, the caller viewed a black woman canvassing as a potential threat. Some people will always see what makes us different before they see the common good that unites us.

When you know who you are, it is easier to stay the course.

I didn't allow this to upset me or take me out of character. Instead, I used it as an opportunity to educate and inspire. When you know who you are, it is easier to stay the course. I've never gotten involved in disputes over who people say I am or what people say

I've done because I know. I know, and the people that need to know, know. When it comes to elected officials and campaigning, people forget that candidates are people too. They have families, children, and grandchildren. Saying damaging things about a person can be hurtful. I've never gotten stuck in a resentful mindset because I know that line of thinking will quickly derail the process and hinder your results.

Stay consistent, and the truth will emerge.

People will speak up for you when your character speaks for itself. Some people will quickly advocate on my behalf because they've watched my life, and they know I live a life of integrity. I can't say it enough; consistent character validates your reputation. Michelle Obama says it best "when they go low, we go high." My history is saturated with moments where I've taken the high road. Taking the high road is not situational, it is a lifestyle I've learned to live.

I've taught this principle to my children. I've told them to stay high and not go low when someone does something to try to bring them to a level they are not on. Simply put, if they lived in an apartment building on the ninth floor, and someone on the second floor is insulting them, there is no reason to respond. It doesn't even make sense to engage, because that floor is not where you live. You cannot live responding to insults developed out of low-level thinking. My words of instruction to them their entire life have been, "you don't have to respond to everything."

Our son was a senior in high school, and his basketball team had just won their high school basketball state championship. It was the first championship for his school. He was a skilled player and set three records during the tournaments. He had a stellar season. When it ended, there were only four months left until graduation. During his senior year, his dad and I purchased him a Pontiac Grand-AM. He was a responsible young man, and he proved to us that we could trust him.

A few weeks after the season ended, he didn't come home one night from work. I made the typical calls to his friends, and no one had seen him. I called one of his close friends, and he wasn't home either. At that moment, I knew something was up. I started calling the hospitals and checked with the police to see if there had been a car accident or another incident, and no one knew anything. Our country has been devastated by the violent loss of black men by their own hands or another. There was a reasonable cause for alarm when a young, black boy hadn't returned home after work.

I called a friend of ours who was a captain with the police department to see if he could look into it. He looked up my son's name and told me that he had been arrested and charged with substantial battery, which is a felony. None of this made sense to me because it did not fit who I knew my son to be. Substantial battery or assault of any kind did not match his character. Our friend explained to us that it looked like our son was involved in a fight with someone who had received extensive injuries. I couldn't believe it. A child who had never been suspended from school, was now charged with a felony? When I say it didn't match the behavior of my son, I'm not saying it because that's what all mothers say. This child had literally never been in any kind of trouble. Yes, things do happen, but I knew there had to be more to the story.

I had to go down and bail him out and wait for a court date to find out what the next steps would be. When the truth finally came out, we learned that our son and his friends were at an apartment of another friend playing cards. He and one friend (the one he was arrested with) left to go pick up some pizzas with his discounts because he worked at a pizza place. While they were gone, another friend got into a dispute with a neighbor. This dispute had nothing to do with the boys that left to get the pizza. The argument turned into a fight, and the fight was intense.

When they returned, the police were already there and began questioning both boys. They wanted to know if they had a connection to the fight that happened. My son told me one of the officers was a white female. She noticed their high school letter jackets and said to them she did not like athletics. Somehow, from that comment and their continued conversation, she decided to take them downtown for questioning. My son and his friend were kept in jail overnight. When it was all over, the charges against the boys were dropped. It was clear they were not involved and had nothing to contribute to their investigation.

Having an adverse experience like this with the police could have sent my son on a different road, but he knew to stay high. They never saw me get upset about something I didn't do, so he didn't get upset about something he hadn't done. I'm thankful for the teaching he had and his obedience to his parents because, for all I know, that saved his life.

In 2018, I reflected on the experience my son had when I was invited to give the community response during Act II of Dael Oralndersmith's play, *Until the Flood*. This presentation was a depiction of the tragedy of Michael Brown, an 18-year old African American man who was fatally shot by a white officer in Ferguson, Missouri. Tragedies like this pierce the heart of a mother, especially mothers of African American men. The unfortunate reality was that my son could go to work, school, or hang out with friends, and in a moment, become a statistic of a tragic incident.

I was very clear with him in his teenage years, if you ever get stopped by the police, don't move. Don't move your hands and don't say anything. Be obedient, and do whatever they're asking you to do; I want you to come back home. I always reminded him, we can figure out the rest later. I am thankful he listened.

The situation could have been a lot worse had he taken the low road. It's important not to be in the wrong place at the wrong time, but what happens when you're in a place and the wrong thing happens? You can't always control what other people will do, but you can stay the course and control your behavior and response.

Your life is a reflection of your choices.

I've always told my children that the choices you make today, you will live by tomorrow. I allow them to see my life as an example. I don't have a hard life, my body is not run down, and I have not done things that would make this season of my life difficult to live.

There are people that I grew up with that made different choices, and it is reflected in how their lives have turned out. Even if you've gotten off course, you can get back on track. Mistakes happen; in fact, they are inevitable. It's important to remember you can choose not to be defined by them. As long as there is breath in your body, you can get back on course and make your life something you want it to be.

As long as there is breath in your body, you can get back on course.

I look at some of the young women today who drink irresponsibly, smoke illegally, and live the fast life. They may not believe it now, but it ages you. Sometimes you can look at a person and tell when they've made decisions that produced a hard life. Even if they don't look like it, the moment they open their mouth, you can hear it in how they talk. There is an undertone of defeat and despair. It is evident they have not made the best out of the life they've lived. However, there is always hope. I think about my dad. It took him a long time, but he finally got it together before he left this world.

It takes faith to stay the course.

My life has flourished because I've stayed the course. Through it all, my character, my faith, and my integrity are consistent. Almost every adversity there is to see, I've seen. Homelessness, loss, devastation, I've been there. I've been on public assistance. I had a parent who was an alcoholic, and there have been challenges in my family.

I'm sharing my experiences because it doesn't matter what you've suffered, you can still become something you're proud of—faith makes it possible.

Early in our marriage, my husband and I lost our home. It was one of the worst situations ever, but we recovered. There are moments in life that you may lose something. Losing one thing doesn't mean you've lost everything. Since that loss, we've been able to purchase new homes and build a house from the ground up. We've since been the owner of four properties.

When we lost our home, it wasn't the traditional process of foreclosure. It wasn't calculated or something that gave us time to prepare. No, we woke up and there was a placard on the door that said vacate in 48 hours. At this time, I was a stay at home mom, and our growing family survived on my husband's income—unfortunately, an unexpected strike on his depleted our resources. By the time his employment resumed, it was too difficult for us to recover. The mortgage company began the foreclosure proceedings, and with the late payments, interests, and penalties, we could not catch up. Following advice from credible resources, we maintained all the bills we could. We knew the foreclosure would come, and right before Thanksgiving in 1983, we received the notice to vacate.

We had three children at the time, and thankfully my mother had a house that was available to us. It wasn't what we were used to, but I made that place home. Instead of sulking in our misfortune, we started saving money and planning for life on the other side of our loss. I went and put all the furniture I wanted on layaway. I started picking up everything I wanted in my new house. We didn't have a house, and we didn't know where we would live next, but I was preparing us so that we would be ready. I understood just because we didn't have a place to go yet, I knew that at some point, things would be better, and we would have a home. So, I prepared for it — you must make room for what you're asking God to do for you.

My sister, who was in real estate, reached out to me and invited me to come to look at a house. I was hesitant because I thought we weren't ready. We needed to build our savings and make sure we could sustain whatever home we moved into next. Although we were preparing, my faith was still maturing. You have to trust Him with your decisions. God knows you better than you know yourself.

Eventually, I went to look at the house, and it was perfect. I had already bought household items in my favorite colors like mauve and turquoise, and the house matched those colors. It was as if God said because you've stepped out and continued preparing, I've prepared a place for you that's going to be perfect.

We moved into that house and stayed there for 15 years. When you stay the course, you continue to learn and grow. I'm naturally a hard worker, and I will do whatever it takes to get the job done or to accomplish a goal. Even if I have people that can do certain things for me, I'm willing to put the work in myself. If I'm available and I can do it, I will do it. Now, as I gracefully mature in age, wisdom has taught me not to do as much. However, in my youth, I never expected someone else to do something for me that I could do for myself.

God knows you better than you know yourself.

Be committed to your personal growth along the way.

Personal growth, or what some call personal development, is a process of maturity that produces an awareness of who you are. It allows you to see your areas of strength as well as areas in your life that require improvement. An opportunity that allowed me to grow personally is serving as our pastor's secretary for ten years. I was faithful and stayed the course while serving him. He could count on me to complete the tasks he assigned, and many of the skills I developed as the secretary became transferable skills in my personal and professional life.

At a time where it wasn't popular to perfect typing as a skill, I could type 100 words per minute. I didn't develop my typing skills on a fancy keyboard, but on a classic typewriter. When you wanted to begin a new paragraph, you couldn't just hit the enter key a few times. You needed to manually move the paper by roller knobs that were on the side of the typewriter. I'm glad that technology has come a long way. At the same time, I appreciate the critical thinking required to complete simple projects because it reinforced that skill for me.

I practiced punctuality by being prepared before time. My pastor would drop his written sermon off at my house by eight o'clock in the morning. I would type it up on my typewriter and have it ready for him before church started at eleven o'clock. Managing my time well was necessary to complete the task, prepare breakfast for my family, dress myself and three children, and arrive at church on time. Every week I practiced this, I became better and more efficient. In addition to our Sunday morning routine, we attended church every Wednesday and every Friday, faithfully. I had responsibilities as the secretary on each of these days, and I learned to balance my home life and my church life.

In this role, I learned hard lessons of leadership. When faced with challenges, my first response was prayer. I would ask God what I needed to learn by what was happening and seek Him for guidance on how to handle it. Every challenge I faced produced growth. I learned what worked well and what did not. Just because it's the church or what some call ministry, it doesn't eliminate the challenges that come with working with people. It can sometimes magnify them because one may assume that because it is in the faith community that everyone will conduct themselves with Christian character. People in the church have different levels of spiritual discipline and commitment; this is on full display when serving them. Some would bring worldly behaviors into our faith community, such as gossiping, unforgiveness, jealousy, treating each other unkind, and other things not pertaining to godliness. My response needed to mirror the love of God at all times because I represented our pastor, our church, and our God.

Personally and professionally, I grew by staying the course in this area. It strengthened my character, and it taught me that you shouldn't change who you are because of how people respond. I would work in the church and give all I had, and there were moments people did not receive my service. A nasty response from someone would kill my spirit. I had to learn to put on the full armor of God and stand no matter what was before me.

Dealing with the responses of people would feel overwhelming to me at times, and I would operate out of fear. Situations would test my confidence and whether or not I really believed I could do all things through Christ who gives me strength, or was it just something I said. The strength of God allowed me to know that He was fighting for me, and all I needed to do was stay consistent. I could not wear my feelings on my shoulder and fly off the handle because something happened I didn't like. It was not wise for me to take things personally because they were not. Once I finally learned this, I was able to serve in greater capacities because I was no longer distracted.

> *It was not wise for me to take things personally because they were not.*

Working for my pastor began in my twenties, so many of the things I struggled with were age appropriate. I still needed to choose to grow personally and not become stuck, giving responses at the maturity level of a twenty-year-old by the time I turned thirty. Sometimes my voice was overlooked because I was young and working with what we called "seasoned" or older adults. As I am now seasoned, I understand that just because a person is younger than you are, you shouldn't devalue their voice. Many times meaningful contributions can be missed when people become stuck at a person's age, whether they are old or young. I am thankful for those who were experienced enough around me to give me room to grow and guided me with wisdom throughout the process.

You can do all things through Christ.

You can't be afraid to step out in faith and trust what God has given you. Do what He has put inside of you to do. You may not get it right the first time, and you may not get it right all the time. As you step out and do what He has called you to do, the pieces you need will come together. He will use everything you've learned to perfect you in all areas.

Chapter Six

Be Innovative

Develop entrepreneurial skills you can use throughout your life.

"A man's gift maketh room for him, and bringeth him before great men." Proverbs 18:16 (KJV)

If the entire world was to shut down today, what skills do you have to sustain you and your family? Being innovative and developing entrepreneurial skills has equipped me to make a lot with little and given me the advantage to help others do the same. Schools no longer teach many of the skills you need for life. Home economics, shop class, and even trades that were previously available in schools have vanished. I am thankful for every domestic skill I learned growing up. I've recalled each of these abilities, and they have been useful in my life and for my family.

Resourcefulness runs in the family.

From my dad teaching me to fish to my great-grandmother wringing chickens, being resourceful runs through my blood, and I am a beneficiary of that resourcefulness. My mother's family was from Pine Bluff, Arkansas, and our grandfather would take two of us down there every year to see family. My brothers would go one summer and the next summer my sister and I would travel with our grandfather. Those were some of the best times of my childhood. We would leave late at night and have a packed lunch, usually chicken and some sandwiches. Back then, we could not make many stops along the way because it was dangerous for black people to travel from the north to the south without being harassed or questioned.

By daybreak, we would be close to our destination and excited to get out of the car. Our grandfather had several siblings, and they lived in different parts of the south, so we would travel around to see them. During one visit, my great-grandmother wrung a chicken's neck to prepare it for dinner. It was a crazy event, and if you've seen one wrung, I'm sure you've never forgotten it. If you know anything wringing chickens, you must be quick and precise. I watched her grab the chicken by its feet, and let's just say the rest was dinner.

That is not a skill I have. However, if it were a skill I needed to use, I'd use it and make a meal. I remember watching it and being amazed at the process. I've always been one to pay attention to things around me. Asking questions is also crucial to developing your skill set. If you don't know, you can't be afraid to ask.

Skills such as: boiling an egg, how to treat the common cold, taking care of flowers, how to clean a house, or use essential tools, are all relevant and necessary. When these skills become areas of expertise, you can do something with them. I learned to sew and grew into being a seamstress. I began to sew clothes for myself and my children. If they needed an outfit for a special occasion, Christmas, Easter, all of it, I made it. I even made prom dresses for my daughters. The dresses were so impressive their friends wanted to know their seamstress; I was proud to say, it was me, their mom. This produced a stream of income for me because I would make multiple dresses and sell them.

My sewing skills are valuable again in the era of our global pandemic. While sewing may seem like a small task, it is now a coveted talent. At the time of this writing, there is not a vaccine to stop the spread of the coronavirus. Our world went into a mass shortage of personal protective equipment, including medical masks. People were rushing to stores and depleting online selling platforms to protect themselves. Without a pattern on how to make a mask, I combined sewing and creativity to make masks for my family and friends. I donated 100 masks for families with small children and made over 50 masks with graduation designs as gifts for high school seniors.

I'm also a cook. I learned how to make cakes, pies, and special desserts that were not just for my family. I perfected recipes so that I could sell them. Many of us are multi-gifted; we just don't use all the gifts that we have. Sometimes we don't know the gifts are there.

Be Innovative

Other times we can be afraid to use them or not have the support we need to develop them fully.

Use your skills and talents with confidence.

My organizational skills and willingness to do the work birthed the gift of entrepreneurship. My desire to work and explore the gifts of God in me has allowed me to experience opportunities of a lifetime. One of those included managing a major recording group and connecting them to a national platform.

I want to be truly clear that I do not consider myself a singer, or the typical performing group manager. My organization, communication, planning, and management skills were on display, and one of the members of the group took notice. You never know when people are watching you and what opportunities may come from what they see.

He watched me serve others by coordinating events and noticed I did these things well. As his group progressed to a place where they needed support managing the operations, he approached me with the offer. I managed the group for five years, and the skills that I used in other areas transferred seamlessly into the role. Following this experience, other groups wanted me to manage them. However, it was not something I did because I decided

...willingness to do the work birthed the gift of entrepreneurship.

not to commit myself to make this a regular service in my portfolio.

An event that stands out to me while managing them was an opportunity they had to sing backup for Michael Bolton. One of the requirements for us to fulfill the contract was that we needed 12 singers in the group. Upon signing, I made sure we could satisfy everything they were asking, and on the day of the concert, one of the singers backed out. I did not panic, I went into action, and when I could not find a replacement—I became the replacement. Never in a million years did I picture myself as a member of the group singing behind a major recording artist, but I did.

Share your gifts with others.

Over the years, I've connected with all types of different people, and as you have seen, I've maintained those relationships. You will meet many kinds of people along your journey. I can't say it enough—stay connected to them. You never know when your paths will cross again.

With all the skills I have, I've always found a way to give back through public service. In every season of my life, I've volunteered and served. In my home, community, church, my kids' school, social arenas, and more. Public service should not be a burden. It is a gift we give honoring the ways others have served us.

When serving others, do not do it for money. You must understand that value extends beyond monetary compensation. You can build long standing relationships through public service. Service allows you a platform to grow and develop your gifts. Some people will do anything to try and get in front of who they think are the right people when all they have to do is serve. Find somewhere to offer your gift and expect nothing in return.

There are some places I've offered my gift, and it was rejected. That's okay. It didn't stop me from trying. People may not understand the work that you put into making something great but put the work in any way. I remember hosting fundraisers and running events, and I would be so involved in the process. I would do everything I could to make sure it was perfect, and there would be one thing that was off. Perhaps someone's name was missed, or something didn't turn out right, and it would crush me. I had to grow out of that.

> *Find somewhere to offer your gift and expect nothing in return.*

At this point in my life, I understand it is what it is. I'm not going there, and I refuse to let people or situations get me emotionally engaged when I know I've done my best. For some people, your best will never be good enough. It doesn't mean that it wasn't your best.

Around the age of 40, something in me changed. It was like a light came on. I was at a place in my life where I knew who I was. I was comfortable with who I was becoming, and I quit recess. In other words, I was done playing games, especially those that were immature and attempted to bait me into insecurity. My children were 12, 16, and 20, and they were at a stage where they could be self-sufficient. I had been married for 22 years with peaks and valleys. I was putting my skills to use and loving my life. My gifts were making room for me, and I was thriving.

During this time, I was the executive director of a housing agency, and the board president wanted to micromanage me. For some reason, she wanted to make my job harder than it needed it to be. At this point in my life, I was not afraid to walk away. I was good at my job, and I did not need to be micromanaged. You must arrive at a place of maturity where you know your value, you are sure of who you are, and you are unafraid to live out your purpose. I left that job and never looked back; this did not hinder nor deter my life. My life got better and continues to get better. You don't have to subject yourself to the abuse of someone who is intimidated by who you are. Be who you are and be proud of it.

If you are stuck in a job that leaves you unfulfilled, or you know you are not living out what's inside you — you may need to do something different. Of course, I tell everybody, you never leave a job until you have another job. I also say, don't be afraid to try something new. Trust what you've got in you. Don't let your gifts die in the valley of your life. Daybreak is bound to happen, and the valley's don't last forever. I think of all the valley's I've experienced, and what would have happened had I allowed my gifts and my joy to die in the valley? One thing is for sure; I wouldn't be writing this book. My life is an example of perseverance. It's an example of using what you have and what you know, to be the best you can be.

You'll never be stuck dealing with something you don't deserve when you have skills you can use, and you aren't afraid to use them. I think this change happens for most women around the age of 40. There is a liberation that comes with finally knowing who you are and being confident in it. It is the best feeling ever! I call this, stepping into the four R's: relax, renew, retire, and repurpose.

When you relax, you release stress and tension. You are anxious for nothing, and you've mastered the faith to trust God with it all. In the moments of renewal, you have quiet time with God and allow Him to refresh you in the areas that are worn down and tired. We need moments of renewal often.

Retire is the place I'm walking into, but it's not only for those in the season of retirement. Sometimes you need to retire from some things you've been doing that are no longer beneficial for you to keep doing them. Retire and get away from it all so that you can find rest. Once you've done that, you can repurpose, just as

I've repurposed my sewing skills during this season of my life.

There is room for all of your gifts.

I've shared the many ways my gifts have made room for me. I want you to know that there is room for all your gifts too. You never have to compete with anyone or try to force a space for yourself. Continue serving, being consistent, and showing up. You will notice opportunities emerge in ways you've never dreamed of or imagined—simply because you've made yourself available to share your gifts with others.

Chapter Seven

Have Faith
Secure your faith in God, who knows the plans for your life.

"For I know the thoughts that I think toward you, saith the Lord, thoughts of peace, and not of evil, to give you an expected end" Jeremiah 29:11 (KJV)

This scripture captures the sentiments of my heart. God knows his thoughts toward us and His plans for us, and they are good. Everything I have and everything I've obtained is because of God.

I am the first in my family and my community to achieve some of my life accomplishments. I offer them all up to God because, without Him, they would not be possible. People ask me all the time; how did you do it? How do you continue to do it? I remind them, it's my faith that keeps me grounded.

I often say that things don't bother me. In a sense, I live life unbothered. It doesn't mean that things haven't happened or won't continue to happen; however, when they do, I remain confident that God has a plan. Confidence in His plan has kept me consistent in my faith. I've never stopped being who He called me to be. I believe His thoughts toward me are good, and He delights in fulfilling some of my heart's desires.

I've always longed to see the world.

There is nothing more enjoyable to me than traveling and experiencing the beauty of the world God created. I am so fortunate that I've had the opportunity to do this through vacations, birthday celebrations, and educational opportunities. I'd seen pictures of Hawaii and always wanted to go. I have a good friend who traveled to Hawaii often and extended the invitation to my husband and me. Their invitation also included lodging. All we needed to do was pay for our airfare. Delighted by the offer, it was music to my ears, and I thought it would work out perfectly. We didn't purchase our tickets right away but planned to buy them later.

As it got closer to the time for us to go, the cost of the airfare was much higher than what we expected. If we could have driven to Hawaii, my husband would have preferred that method of travel versus flying. Considering this, I wanted to find a flight with few connections and a short duration. Due to the cost of the tickets, this trip to Hawaii did not work out.

Sometimes you may have a desire to do something, but if it is not the right time or things don't line up the way they should, you must be okay with waiting. Learning to wait is a life skill, and it is valuable beyond planning vacations.

Eight years later, we finally made it to Hawaii for the first time, and the conditions were right. I planned the trip, and I was able to get a flight that took us directly from Chicago to Hawaii. I was even able to use my hotel points to book our stay. We stayed right on the ocean. We participated in the luau, and also took a chartered boat into the crystal blue water. Everything lined up just right, and our first visit was incredible.

The second time we traveled to Hawaii, we went on a romantic dinner cruise. The most exciting thing we did was our helicopter ride. They asked us if we wanted the doors on or off. Right away, the cautious nature of my husband said to keep them on, but I wanted my door off. I asked the driver if he could take my door off, and he did. My philosophy was we were already in the air, door on or off—it really didn't matter. I also didn't want a restricted view. We flew over where they filmed Jurassic Park, and it was exhilarating.

We have photos of our experience in Hawaii, and they are gorgeous. Still, they do not adequately capture the beauty of the experience. It is one of the loveliest places I've ever seen. The flowers, the water, were all breathtaking. The weather was perfect, when it rained, it sprinkled. The people were amazing. It was worth the wait and is an experience I will never forget and will take as often as I can.

Oceans away, relationships still matter.

For my 60th birthday, I wanted to go to Paris. It was my dream. All the planning for my party was Parisian themed, the invitations, the cake, the decorations, everything. When people asked what I wanted for my birthday, I told them they could donate to my Paris trip. All I wanted to do that year was to go to Paris.

I didn't make it to Paris the year I turned 60, so my family brought Paris to me. The celebration was beautiful and encouraged me to make my Paris trip a reality. Know what you want in life, and make a list of the places you want to go. Once you do this, make a plan to get there. Three years later, I made it to Paris, and it too was worth the wait.

My husband opted to go, and he wanted to plan it with me. Together we decided to make it a cruise. We flew to Los Angles to connect with our Viking cruise port. We had a first-class cabin, with a patio, and all the amenities we desired. Each day the cruise ship docked and let us off to explore a new city. We visited where artists lived and worked experiencing history right before our eyes. I've seen paintings by Vincent van Gogh never thinking I would walk the streets he walked on.

Know what you want in life...

This trip was another opportunity to reveal the gift of maintaining relationships. A good friend had recently lost her husband and shared with me a friend of her son moved to Paris after his service in the military. She told me he was street a musician traveling to different towns, and he also performed in some of the local clubs. Certain streets in Paris are like live stages with music, theater, paintings, and all sorts of artistic beauty. My friend gave me a description of this young man and told me his name was Rene Miller. She said if you see him, tell him hello.

We got off the ship at one of the ports to walk around near the Cathédrale Notre-Dame de Paris. My husband and I visited some of the shops, and we walked past a musician playing on the street. At first, I didn't think anything of it and kept walking. When we came out of the shop, I stopped and listened to the young man play, and when he finished, I asked him his name. To my surprise, it was him. I asked if he knew my friend, and right away, he said, yes. I shared with him that she wanted me to tell him hello. Although our homes are oceans apart, that moment was surreal. There was an instant connection through our mutual relationship that brought tears to our eyes.

He immediately began to play a song for my friend. I recorded it for her to hear. He sang words to the song "Just a Closer Walk With Thee." What are the odds that all the way in Paris, I would connect with this young man who would bring a sweet song of healing for my friend in her loss? Who knew? God knew. It was all by His design.

The young man invited my husband and me to come to his show, but our ship was sailing toward the next city that evening. There are so many moments like this that have existed in my life, where I know it was the hand of God, allowing things to happen. I sent the song directly to my friend, and she couldn't believe I found him. I didn't find him; God did.

Multicultural experiences are a gift.

Another experience of a lifetime was the three weeks I spent in Japan through the Fulbright education program. The experience was paid in full. They flew me from Milwaukee to San Francisco and from San Francisco to Narita, Japan, and finally from Narita to Tokyo. I had a private room at the Hyatt and also had a chance to stay with a Japanese family to experience their culture. It was the first time I had been away for an extended period where you couldn't just go home if you wanted too. I was worlds away from my backyard.

One night in Japan, there was an earthquake. I felt something that shook me so hard I fell out the bed but didn't think anything of it. I had never experienced an earthquake, so I had no point of reference to what was happening. When I woke up that morning, everyone was talking about what happened the night before and asking did I feel the earthquake. I knew then what happened, and it prepared me for the aftershocks.

Japan was a culturally rich experience, and I would love to go back. On my last day in Tokyo, I visited a souvenir store where I met a beautiful Japanese woman. There was a bench in the middle of the store. I sat down to take in the experience, and after a moment, the woman sat down next to me. Her English wasn't the best, and neither was my Japanese.

Kindness has its own language, and through that, we understood each other well.

I got up to walk around the store and as I headed toward the door, she met me with a gift bag. The beautiful bag contained a porcelain chopstick holder and a scarf. She appreciated my interest in her culture, and I was thankful she was willing to share it with me. When I brought the gift home, I took it to Creative Enterprises, a local framing shop, and had it framed. When people give you things, don't leave them in a bag or a box. Use the gifts or figure out a way to cherish them.

Kindness has its own language.

If I have learned anything in my travels, it is that the culture in the United States is very different from cultures across the world. Things like stealing and drunk driving are not commonly accepted. I remember checking out of the hotel in Japan and noticed a large area roped off. Behind the rope were cameras, jewelry, clothes, and things that people left behind. Hotel staff would gather the items and put them in a space for people who came back looking for their things. I admired that because it meant if you left something behind, it would still be there. There is so much we can learn from other cultures and experiencing them firsthand, is eye-opening.

If you desire to travel the world, do it.

I traveled to Spain taking my mother and daughter with me. Not only do I desire to see the world, but I wanted to provide them an international experience as well. Knowing the cost associated with taking the three of us out of the country, I understood I needed to be resourceful. I was looking for a way to raise money for this trip and knew of an artist in Georgia who made beautiful paintings that were popular at the time. I owned a few of them and knew that he was looking to create awareness of his art. I contacted him and asked if I could market and sell his paintings, he agreed. I financed the entire trip through art sales.

Anything you want to do, you can make a plan to do it. I always have. I don't believe there is a goal you can set that is out of your reach. If you set your mind to do it and ask God to give you a strategy to accomplish it, I believe He will do just that.

My travels have shown me the awesomeness of God and the beauty of this world. If you can travel, I recommend that you go and see the world. I think of the places I've seen in books and how God has allowed my dreams of travel to become a reality.

Retirement is a gift to repurpose.

I've been making moves and preparing myself to enjoy the things I want to do when my retirement begins. For me, I see the next season in my life as a gift to repurpose my skills and passions through new avenues of influence. While my professional journey may look different, my commitment to serving others and dedication to my core values will always remain.

In 2014 we moved to Brown Deer, Wisconsin. Two years later, we decided to invite our neighbors who lived around our block to join us on our patio for refreshments. While we fellowshipped in our backyard, someone suggested we host a block party, and that I should plan it. Right away I said, "No,"

Following the refreshments in our backyard that summer, I decided to turn my "no" to hosting the block party into a "yes." A few weeks before the event, I canvassed the total distance of our suburban area, inviting everyone to attend. I also sent an email to all the Trustees in Brown Deer, Wisconsin, to encourage them to participate in the block party to meet the constituents. I didn't get a response. On the day of the event, none of the trustees showed up.

After the event, I decided to start attending the meetings. I would sit in the audience and observe as all the trustees would come in, go to their seats, discuss the business at hand and never acknowledge my presence. After a few months of listening to the conversation, I was shocked by some of the decisions made. I spoke with my husband and daughter about what they thought about me running for office. Running for public office had been suggested to me before, and this time felt right.

Around this time, I attended the Congressional Black Caucus Convention in Washington, D.C. I participated in a dinner where I sat at a table with several influential women from Milwaukee. I shared with them that I was thinking about running for office. After some discussion, they all agreed that it was a good idea for me to run and made a commitment to support me. We jokingly talked about using the trending hashtag from Meghan Markle and Prince Harry #BeTheOne.

I am thankful for the women that rallied around me, supported me, and believed that I could be the one. When I returned home, I filed the necessary paperwork to be on the ballot that coming November. My neighbors helped me get the support of over 100 signatures within a week when I only needed 20 to get on the ballot.

I am now the Village President, and it all stemmed from my initiative to build relationships. I am the first woman of color to hold this position in the history of our city. During my campaign, I rallied our community bringing people with differences to the table for real conversations. I walked miles connecting and meeting with constituents. Bringing people together wasn't new territory to me because I've always been a connector and valued the power of relationships.

Throughout my life, I've been successful in many endeavors because of relationships. I've been recognized by my local community with several honors, including; Woman of Influence by the Milwaukee including; Woman of Influence by the Milwaukee Business Journal, 2019 Leading Lights—Children's Service Award from St. Francis Children's Center, Edith N. Finlayson Community Service Award for Community Service from Milwaukee Chapter of Links, James Howard Baker Community Service from Community Brainstorming, Pastors United Community Service Award, and Alumni Award from Riverside/Rufus King Association. While I've never expected anything in return for serving others, my heart is overwhelmed by every gift, honor, and award.

Black Mamas Rock.

I can honestly say it is well with my soul. There is so much more on the horizon for me. I have so much more to give. I'm creating my legacy every day. I fell in love with the theme of Black Girls Rock. The more I thought about it, the more I realized that, yes, black girls do rock! So do black mamas! We are pillars in our homes and communities. We take care of our children and our families. We inspire others. We are teachers, nurses, hairdressers, cooks, counselors, and so much more.

I'm building a business and a legacy my daughters and granddaughters can carry on. Black Mamas Rock is going to inspire women everywhere. Through this effort, I will remind black mamas to use all their gifts, be proud of who they are, and leave a legacy worth remembering. I'm excited that the Black Mamas Rock movement will follow the release of this book.

I realize that I am no longer standing on the shoulders of those before me. I am now squaring my shoulders for others to stand on.

So, what's next for Wanda Montgomery? I think that's for the Lord to decide. He's done such an amazing job of orchestrating my life so far, and I look forward to seeing how else He plans to get His glory out of my life.

References

Russell, Joyce E. A. "Career Coach: The Power of Using a Name." The Washington Post, WP Company, 12 Jan. 2014, www.washingtonpost.com/business/capitalbusiness/career-coach-the-power-of-using-a-name/2014/01/10/8ca03da0-787e-11e3-8963-b4b654bcc9b2_story.html.

"Wanda." SheKnows, 22 Aug. 2018, www.sheknows.com/baby-names/name/wanda/.

"Alcohol Use Disorder." National Institute on Alcohol Abuse and Alcoholism, U.S. Department of Health and Human Services, 31 Jan. 2020, www.niaaa.nih.gov/alcohol-health/overview-alcohol-consumption/alcohol-use-disorder

MEMORIES FROM JAPAN...

"KINDNESS HAS ITS OWN LANGUAGE"

PROFESSIONALS & FRIENDS

DR. EVE HALL
President/CEO Milwaukee Urban League

ANGELA ADAMS
VP of Community Relations, Goodwill Industries

WANDA J. MONTGOMERY
Director of Community Partnerships, Children's Wisconsin

SISTER INSPIRING SISTERS

TAMMY SAFFOLD, KAREN CHESIR, VICTORIA BROOKS,
WANDA J. MONTGOMERY,
PATRICIA SAFFOLD, MILDRED COBY, SANDY JONES
NOT PICTURED: APRIL HOLLAND & APRIL MULLINS

LIFETIME FRIENDS

VICTORIA BROOKS,
APRIL MULLINS,
WANDA J. MONTGOMERY

GOLDEN GIRLS

MARY NICHOLAS-OBLIGACION, VALERIA NORWOOD, CAROLYN MOULTRIE, WANDA J. MONTGOMERY

Friends, Family, and Lifetime Relationships

FRIENDS IN LOVE & MARRIAGE

MELVIN & BARBARA MEDCALF
FLOYD & WANDA J. MONTGOMERY

NATIONAL BLACK CHILD DEVELOPMENT INSTITUTE
COMMUNITY SERVICES AWARD

DIMITRIUS HUTCHERSON, BOARD CHAIR, NBCDI
WANDA J. MONTGOMERY
TOBEKA GREEN, PRESIDENT & CEO, NBCDI
CINDRA TAYLOR, PRESIDENT, BCDI-ATLANTA

FRIENDS UNTIL THE END

IN HONOR OF ROSETTA WILLIAMS.
My dear friend who passed away in February of 2014 and trusted me as the executor of her estate.

WOMEN OF INFLUENCE
LINK SISTERS

WANDA J. MONTGOMERY,
NANCY JOESPH,
ERICKAJOY DANIELS

WOMEN OF INFLUENCE
AWARD 2017

WANDA J. MONTGOMERY

THE GRAY LEGACY

PERCY AND BESSIE GRAY, SR.;
FELICIA BOURRAGE, 1953; WANDA J. MONTGOMERY, 1954;
PERCY GRAY, JR., 1956; BRYANT GRAY, 1957;
MARK GRAY, 1958,; CLAUDIA GRAY, 1960;
ZACHARY GRAY, 1961; TAMMY SAFFOLD, 1963
LASONIA MCGEE, 1972

THE MONTGOMERY LEGACY

FLOYD & WANDA MONTGOMERY;

MARCELLE & PHILLIP, SR. PHILLIP, JR. HADDIX;

ADRIAN & CHAUNCEY, KAMILLE AND KYE MONTGOMERY POLO (dog);

CANDACE MONTGOMERY HAMILTON (dog)

FOReVER IN LOVE

FLOYD & WANDA J. MONTGOMERY

INFLUENCE:
IT'S MORE THAN A POSITION

WANDA J. MONTGOMERY & CHIEF JUDGE MAXINE WHITE